Take the Quantum Leap

~INTO ABUNDANCE~

A GUIDE TO THE GOOD LIFE

C.W. PICKETT

Mu Shin Press

If you have not linked yourself to true emptiness
You will never understand
The Art of Peace

© Copyright 2017 Mu Shin Press
ISBN 13: 978-0-692-84883-8

All rights reserved.

No part of this publication may be reproduced in any manner without prior written permission of the author, except in the case of brief quotations embodied in reviews, or as protected by law. cpickett@wyoming.com

DISCLAIMER

This publication is the culmination of many years of research. Reference to published works by other authors are sufficiently notated in the Bibliography. The narrative of <u>The Stockdale Paradox</u> is a paraphrase of the original work. The direct quotes in the selection are written exactly as recorded.

DEDICATION

To my Father, who taught me that

Success comes in CANS
Failure comes in CANT'S

~Martin Walter~

CONTENTS

FORETHOUGHTS 1

WHAT IS ABUNDANCE? 1
HEALTHY, WEALTHY, AND WISE 1

CHAPTER 1 9

HOBSON'S CHOICE 9
THIS HORSE OR NONE 9

CHAPTER 2 19

THE STOCKDALE PARADOX 19
FACE YOUR BRUTAL REALITY 19

CHAPTER 3 25

THE CYCLE OF NEEDS 25
SECURE IN OUR HOMES 25

CHAPTER 4 33

POSITIVE SELF IMAGING 33
TAKING ACTION 33

CHAPTER 5 — 41

THE TALKING STICK — 41
LISTENING WITH EMPATHY — 41

CHAPTER 6 — 51

YUIMARU - RECIPROCITY — 51
HELP THY NEIGHBOR — 51

CHAPTER 7 — 61

A MAN OF PEACE — 61
WHAT IS ZEN? — 61

CHAPTER 8 — 77

FAITH AND FORGIVENESS — 77
RELEASE THE GRUDGE — 77

AFTERTHOUGHTS — 83

DO WHAT YOU LOVE — 83

You must never confuse faith that you will prevail in the end – which you can never afford to lose – with the discipline to confront the most brutal facts of your current reality, whatever that might be."

~Admiral James Stockdale~

FORETHOUGHTS

WHAT IS ABUNDANCE?

HEALTHY, WEALTHY, AND WISE

> Do not fail to learn from the pure voice
> of an ever-flowing mountain stream
> splashing over the rocks.
>
> ~*The Art of Peace*~

ABUNDANCE.
WHAT IS IT?   HOW DO YOU FIND IT?
HOW DO YOU KNOW WHEN YOU HAVE FOUND IT?

In the late 1980's, there was a television series called The *Quantum Leap*. Doctor Sam Beckett devised a time-travel machine and was forced to use it before it was thoroughly tested. The machine backfired, and he found himself in another body, traveling from life to life, looking for his way back home. His one helper was Al, a holographic image seen only by Dr. Beckett.

This book is not about time travel, nor is it science fiction. When a person travels from one level of consciousness to another, they are taking the Quantum Leap, a giant leap of faith into their metaphorical "other world;" the world that exists exclusively in personal dreams and ambitions.

Where is this other world, this life of abundance? People are searching for truths, for a way of living not fraught with violence and drama. Many books are written on how to live a better life, nearly to the point of information overload. This book is different. You cannot think yourself thin, nor can you dream your way into riches. The work ethic of "no work, no food," applies to making your life better, as well. If you do not apply the energy and time necessary to build a better life for yourself, you will not succeed. The ideas presented here are not my own, but gathered over the years through education, research, experience, and the school of hard knocks.

Intentionally written to be thought provoking, my book is not intended to be a sit-down one-time read for a couple of hours. It is my goal that you stop and reflect on an insight, or perhaps a quote will help you along the way. The ideas presented here have helped me through difficult times, and I hope you will refer to this book often, just as I did while writing it.

My books are intended to pass on worthwhile knowledge that readers can apply to their lives. Knowledge is useless unless passed on. Without sharing what we have learned, education and knowledge sit in our brains and stagnate. What you read in these pages is a compilation of universal truths and of knowledge passed down through time; truths that light the dark corners of our souls.

Let us begin the journey with this simple statement.

Your thoughts make you. Think positive thoughts and you will have a positive life.

Much is written on the subject. Through the centuries, many people have told us our thoughts lead the way: Norman V. Peale, Aristotle, William James, Myomoto Musashi, Admiral James Stockdale, Maya Angelou, and Mother Theresa are examples. People such as these discover universal truths and pass them on as their legacy. For the purposes of this book, they are called Quantum People. Their experiences led them to abundance and self-fulfillment - their lives shine a bright beacon for us to follow.

"But wait!" you ask. "If thinking positive thoughts is all it takes, then why is there poverty and chronic illness? Why have people suffered through the ages with slavery and oppression?" If all you had to do was wish, would these conditions exist? What poor man hasn't dreamed of wealth? What dying man hasn't yearned for a return to his health and vigor?

Visualize your dream, imagine it coming to life. Is it an impossible dream to see yourself thin? Is it impossible to find happiness? Are we fooling ourselves by imagining a better life is waiting for us if we try a little harder? How true is this advice the Quantum People give? For instance, is it possible to *Think and Grow Rich*?

To write this book, these questions, and many others, needed to be answered. What good is advice if it is poppycock? There are many components to living a successful life, and each person's definition of success is different. The path you chose is your path, you find people along the way who are compatible with you, but the path is yours and only yours. For the most part, it is possible to choose the path of your life, but some choices are made for you, whether you like them or not. Your life is defined by how you rebound from unpleasant experiences or outcomes.

All it takes to start a dream is to put a thought into your brain and then forget about it. Physical motion measures our sense of time, but in the universe, and therefore our thoughts, time has no boundaries or measurement. Life's lessons happen when we are receptive to the point, and not a moment earlier. "Why didn't I think of that sooner?" Now is when your mind is eager for the idea, and you didn't have enough information to act "sooner."

Have you ever done the exercise, "If I were to die in six months, what could I do with the time I have remaining?" One of the items on my list was to write a book, which I wrote down, tucked the paper away, and forgot about. Fifteen years later, after publishing my first book, I rediscovered the paper.

Unknown to me at the time, a thought was anchored in my brain and left to grow on its own. Over the years, this commitment stayed as a niggling voice in my head, the ideas turned into words on paper, and one day, a book appeared. At the time of the original thought, there was no time limit, and I did it as a challenge to see if vision-and-it-will-happen worked, and if I would ever complete the task. At that time in my life, I was as skeptical of seeing-is-believing as you probably are now. The book did not write itself, of course. What wrote the book were my physical actions of researching the topic and putting the words on paper.

Nevertheless, a remote dream turned into an idea strong enough to weather life's challenges and become real.

Do not give up when life isn't happening on your time schedule. Your job is to plant the seeds and then let the Universe do the work. Your idea will massage and grow in your subconscious until one day it will become a reality. But only if you give it room to grow. If things aren't happening on your time line and you plead, beg, and grovel because you want quick results, your idea will slip away.

Life is an adventure, a process. A process that takes a lifetime. The recipe involves positive thoughts, gratitude, visualizing, faith, and *patience*. Positive thinking in and of itself does not produce a single result. What produces results is action. As we will see in Chapter 5, Positive Self-Imaging, the bridge between thought and action, is discipline.

Discipline of mind and body, of habits, and of daily living. When thinking positively, a person uses discipline to reign in the negative thoughts when they start. There is no room for "I will never ..." "I will never get well." "I will never walk again." "I will never..."

It is not fully possible to absolutely, without question, control our thoughts and our destiny. It is wrong to assume we completely control our lives. We do control our destiny to a point, but there are outside influences and internal beliefs that also determine the direction of our lives.

If you are living in trauma, you may see the world as scary. Thoughts alone will not change that. You will not suddenly wake up one day and see the world as a safe place. Be wary of the charlatans who sell the idea of "thinking positive" without offering a solution of how to do this.

You are not a failure if you cannot think yourself rich. People fail when striving toward a fulfilling life because they do not have the knowledge or the tools for success.

My book has practical and simple techniques for developing skills that lead to living an abundant life. There is a chapter on how to improve your self-image, another on the importance of listening. No book of this kind is complete without a chapter on meditation, but here you will find a method different from the rest, and it only takes a few minutes a day. You will find yourself doing this simple, calming practice whenever you have the chance. Now you can drift off to sleep with your last thoughts of qi, your life force, slowly meandering throughout your body. With practice over time, you will be able to use qi energy to heal hot spots and relieve pain.

You will read about people who overcame their adversity and turned it into a peak experience, a life-defining moment, and lived a long and fulfilling life. We will explore choices that are not choices, the cycle of needs we live by, and why some people are more resilient than others. Each chapter focuses on a person or group of people whose faith gives us hope that anyone who wants to can find their authentic life.

The people in this book are real. They arrived at their philosophy of better living through trial and tribulation. The idea is to present their legacies, and by following their path, the reader may also find abundance and self-fulfillment.

What is good living? How do you know when you have found abundance? Let us first look at choices that are not really choices.

CHAPTER 1

HOBSON'S CHOICE

THIS HORSE OR NONE

Think of your customer's needs, not your own.
Create the image of yourself as someone who cares about the
customer, not about the customer's money,
and you will always do well.
~*Norman Vincent Peale*~

WHAT IS YOUR PERSONAL BELIEF FOR BEING ON THIS EARTH? Some people think if they do not resolve their conflicts in this life, they have another chance in another time. Others have the opinion that goodness or badness is resolved in eternal heaven or hell. Still others believe we only have one life to live, and what happens after death does not matter. What we do and how we treat people in this life is all we have. We have only one life to reconcile our wrongs, and this is the goal of our existence.

Whatever your personal belief, one thing is for sure, this is a difficult life punctuated with moments of triumph and celebration. Joys, sorrows, travesties, accomplishments; life is full of twists and turns, happiness and sadness. Imagine a life that is static; unchanging, never moving, the same routine every day, day in and day out. No love, no hate. No color.

Personal boundaries determine what we can and cannot tolerate, but even then, our character and stamina are tested at the most inopportune times. Just when life is going the way we want it to, invariably a hiccup occurs in the carefully laid order, and we are forced to adjust our priorities. Decisions are difficult. Do you take the high road or the low road; or do absolutely nothing and take neither road?

We make choices daily, hourly, by the minute. We choose who to live with, what to eat, and how to spend money. How many times a day you make decisions? We often don't realize we are deciding, it just comes as an automatic response. Many decisions, though, require forethought and sacrifice. We make decisions based on emotion, perception, and state of mind in a fraction of a second.

We unknowingly make life-changing commitments when we are tired, hungry, and intoxicated. Until now, this lack of self-control was gauged as a weakness, a character flaw. We are led to believe if you work hard enough you can change your behavior of poor problem-solving. Change is not easy. You fail because you do not know how to make the change. But with a plan, a formula, a systematic approach, any goal is achievable, including the goal of gaining better self-control.

Radishes, donuts, and horseshoes - and self-control? What a crazy combination! Not so crazy if you consider radishes and donuts are common foods used in studies of self-control. The relevance of horseshoes is explained further on.

Scientists enjoy tempting their subjects with foods; the radish is hot and unappealing to many people, easy to turn down. But donuts! Who can turn down a donut? Test subjects were given one or the other and told not to eat the treat. The subjects who resisted the impulse to eat the donuts showed remarkably lower levels of self-control after the taste test than the ones who were told not to eat the radishes. Not surprisingly, the subjects who were given both the radish and donut, and could choose which one to eat, did the best when tested for self-control after their treat! (DeWall, 2013).

Energy stores are depleted after an emotionally or mentally taxing experience. Resisting a tempting food or engaging in a trying conversation is exhausting, and we must take the time to replenish, physically and mentally.

When our mental reserves are diminished, we make poor decisions. What was the state of your body and mind the last time you lost your temper or made a decision you later regretted?

We fall in love after a long night on the town. We cause rifts in our relationships when we are tired and cranky. We yell at our family when we are most fatigued.

When the body is out of metabolic balance, such as an autoimmune disease, the reserves meant for decision-making go to the imbalance. Staying awake for twenty-four hours is the same as drinking alcohol all night. Most violence occurs between 10 p.m. and 2 a.m. Alcohol is involved in forty-percent of late-night violent crimes (DeWall, 2013).

At the end of the day, instead of home in bed, an out-of-control person is mentally fatigued, tired, hungry, and most likely intoxicated.

Mental energy can be strengthened. Self-control is not a character trait, but a skill. A skill that can be learned and improved upon.

HOW TO GAIN BETTER SELF-CONTROL

~ Walk backwards with your eyes closed.
~ Use only your non-dominant hand for a week.
~ Check your posture often.
~ Be mindful of your actions.
~ Regulate your speech.
~ Keep your personal history to yourself.
~ Be pleasant and respectful.
~ Avoid energy-depleting people.
~ Fill your stores before energy-depleting events.
~ Take time to recharge after a stressful encounter.

By making a conscious effort to monitor and regulate your actions, you are building your self-control mental muscle. Once you become aware of how your body reacts when it becomes depleted, you can take simple actions to build it back up. Better self-control, better decisions.

There are times, though, when choices do not seem like a choice. Sometimes we are presented with a situation that does not have a positive outcome. Or we have a problem that appears to have only one answer, and other options are not acceptable. Here is what horseshoes, decisions, and self-control have in common. We call this Hobson's Choice.

During the centuries before the car, horses were the lifeblood of the people in many cultures. Imagine American history without the horse. What a rich piece of culture surrounds this magnificent animal!

The person most integral to the horse's well-being was the blacksmith. Called different names in different cultures; smithy, blacksmith, farrier, ironsmith, iron forger; since the time of early man-made weapons, a competent blacksmith was highly respected, in high demand, and played an important role in the life of the community.

Blacksmiths worked over a hot furnace where they melted and pounded iron into many shapes, including horseshoes. A horseshoe is a U-shaped piece of metal nailed onto the horse's hooves to protect them from cracking and wearing down from hard riding, rocks, and pavement, and prevents the horse from becoming lame. A broken hoof on a horse is like a human splitting a toenail to the quick, but much more serious.

A blacksmith also kept horses to rent and sell. When a traveler needed a fresh horse, he stopped at the local stable to leave his horse and rent or buy another. Like a car salesman, or a rent-a-car service, today. The difference is horses have a heart, not an engine, and need to rest between rides.

Thomas Hobson was a blacksmith who lived in Oxford, England in the mid-1800s. He had a lucrative business as a blacksmith and rented fresh horses to students from nearby Oxford University, and to travelers in the area. Being an astute businessman, he developed his blacksmithing business into a healthy transportation business. He believed in treating all his customers equally, and only rented or sold the freshest horse. Each customer was given his place in line, and when his turn came, he was given the most rested horse in the stable.

THIS HORSE OR NONE

>A man came into Hobson's stable to buy a horse. Unaware of this equal-treatment policy, the man looked them over, picked his favorite horse, and made Hobson an offer.
>
>"Can't do it," Hobson exclaimed. "That horse isn't for sale!"
>
>The man, taken aback, scratched his head, looked around, pointed to another, and said "Okay, I'll take the dark one."
>
>"Can't do it," Hobson calmly said, "that horse isn't for sale either."
>
>"Well, I thought you sold horses!" The man was getting frustrated.
>
>"I do. You can have the one in the stall closest to the door. The only horse for sale."

Hobson's choice. Only one horse is for sale in the entire stable. Take it or leave it. "This horse or none."

We take the high road because another path is simply not available. Our conscience, morals, values, and principles say, "This is your only choice."

Recognizing choices as a Hobson's Choice frees the mind so as not to dwell on the negatives of the choice. We must accept certain life events and learn to live with the consequences. Life doesn't always give us the freshest horse, and once the decision is made, there are no refunds and no returns.

Perhaps you suffered an accident and have permanent damage. Your life as you knew it is over. A choice? Not a very fresh horse, is it? Nevertheless, you must learn to readjust your life, accept your difficulty, and be grateful for the good things.

Do Quantum People have accidents? Do they become terribly disabled? Does their viewpoint change when this happens? Do accidents only happen to people who don't visualize success? Is it a Hobson's Choice to live in poverty, or to grow up in an abusive home? How can a child have the mindset for anything but fear and shame when she is living in a fearful situation?

Yes, the Quantum People have accidents and horrible experiences. Yet despite their turmoil, they grow into stronger and wiser people than they were before. It is indeed the destination that shows one's mettle and strength.

The journey is just the test.

People frequently transcend hell on earth. There are many stories of people keeping their head in a time of crisis. One story worth sharing is the Stockdale Paradox.

**Confront your brutal reality,
While at the same time, never lose faith
That in the end you will prevail**

~Admiral James Stockdale~

CHAPTER 2

THE STOCKDALE PARADOX

FACE YOUR BRUTAL REALITY

The warrior is always armed with three things:
The radiant sword of pacification;
the mirror of bravery, wisdom, and friendship;
and the precious jewel of enlightenment.

~The Art of Peace~

MAYBE I AM SKEPTICAL BY NATURE and see the glass as half-empty, but the story of the Bear holds true for me.

~ The Bear went over the mountain to see what he could see.

~ The Other Side of the mountain was all that he could see.

Or this one:

~ The grass is always greener until you reach the other side.

These two little ditties say nothing changes, our behaviors are constant, and no matter how hard we want to change, we are chasing after rainbows.

Stop for a moment and consider this question:

How would you feel; physically, mentally, spiritually, and intellectually; if you were given one million dollars!? ($1,000,000). Right now, at this moment, someone knocked on your door and handed you a bag of cash with one-million dollars in it. Not stolen. Honest money. No strings attached. Do with it as you wish. Close your eyes and see this happening.

Describe your emotions. Happy, sad, elated, overjoyed? What are your thoughts? Disbelief? Surprise?

What does abundance feel like? When do you know when the Universe blesses you? Do the heavens open up and shower you with praise? Can you perform miracles and make your wishes come true?

Abundance. Is it spiritual, material, emotional? Tangible or intangible? How do you know when you are wallowing in abundance?

A pleasant thought. Wallowing in abundance! Laying in a field of flowers, not a care in the world. Or sitting in a room filled with gold bars! Pleasant thoughts, but how realistic?

Abundance must feel real. Not a made-up state, but something obtainable. What makes you happy? If imagining gold bars makes you happy, then good luck to you.

If all we need to do is visualize the outcome to realize our dreams, then the rest of this book is unnecessary. But no! Imagination is only the beginning of the journey. Next, you must put action to words.

Once early humans discovered weapons could protect them from predators, they quickly realized sharper and stronger weapons worked better. People have always used intelligence to shape their world, not instinct alone. Certainly, instinct played a role in early man's survival, but no more than it does today.

The human species has not changed over the centuries. We are an upright creature with opposing thumbs and a brain difficult to explain. Scientists estimate the existence of mankind close to 200,000 years ago. One day they will discover for certain where *Homo sapiens* first appeared and when our species started, but whatever the time period, early men and women used intelligence to make life easier.

They studied math, science, geometry, astronomy; we still use the calendar based on the stars. Mathematicians and scientists have long been studying nature, and artisans and engineers apply this knowledge in useful ways. How could someone of low intelligence build a forty-eight-story pyramid made of thousands of limestone blocks, each weighing two-and-a-half tons? After 4000 years, the Great Pyramid of Giza still stands, leaving a puzzle to this day of how the Egyptians built it. They were as technically savvy in their time as we are today with our electronics! As smart as we think we are, we have not evolved much, have we?

The following true story of Admiral Stockdale shows a remarkable example of someone who used intelligence, instinct, and discipline to survive. His leadership and tenacity helped his men through supremely-less-than-abundant conditions. He taught the other prisoners how to survive under torture, endured torture himself, and withstood eight long years as a prisoner of war in one of the most brutal war camps in history. How did he do it?

THE STOCKDALE PARADOX

Admiral James Stockdale, an officer in the Navy, was a prisoner-of-war in the "Hanoi Hilton," the most war brutal camp during the Viet Nam War. Imprisoned for eight years, from 1965 to 1973, he was denied all rights, and had no idea when he would be freed.

He was a leader for the other prisoners and did what he could to assure the men would survive this ordeal as mentally and physically intact as possible. The North Vietnamese were famous for their propaganda, and would often put out media releases showing prisoners in perfect health and well cared for. Admiral Stockdale refused to accept this and beat himself with a stool and disfigured himself with a razor so his captors could not show him as a "well-treated" prisoner.

He and his wife spoke through secret letters and code, knowing if they were discovered he would be tortured. He instituted a step-wise system to help the other prisoners deal with torture; after so many minutes they could say certain things. He also developed a communication system of tapping codes that kept the men from becoming isolated. On the third anniversary of Stockdale's imprisonment, the prisoners swished out "we love you," as they washed the floor with their mops.

"'I never lost faith in the end of the story," he said. "I never doubted not only that I would get out, but also that I would prevail in the end and turn the experience into the defining event of my life, which, in retrospect, I would not trade."

'Who didn't make it out?'

"Oh, that's easy," he said. "The optimists."

"The optimists?" This was confusing, given what he'd said earlier.

"The optimists. Oh, they were the ones who said, 'we're going to be out by Christmas.' And Christmas would come, and Christmas would go. Then they'd say, 'We're going to be out by Easter.' And Easter would come, and Easter would go. And then Thanksgiving, and then it would be Christmas again. And they died of a broken heart" (Collins, 2001).

The Stockdale Paradox says to face your brutal reality while never losing sight of the belief you will meet your goal.

The most profound part of Admiral Stockdale's story is the mindset. "Optimism will kill you," he says. "Christmas comes and goes, and you lose hope. At the very least, the disappointment breaks your heart. At the very worst, you never see another Christmas" (Collins, 2001).

Having optimism does not mean putting on your rose-colored glasses and believing everything is wonderful. Optimism is thinking, "No matter what happens, I can find something to enjoy and find satisfaction."

The lesson here is this: Do not set a date. End dates for a business project are necessary, but life is not a business. Life happens. Setbacks are inevitable when people are involved. Set a date, say in three to six months, but use it as a check-in point, rather than an end-point. Certain life events, like a college graduation, or the birth of a baby, have an end-date, but many goals in life are not as concrete. If you want your life to change completely by Christmas, you will be sorely disappointed. Instead, check in at Christmas and see where you are in your goals. This is the proper use of optimism. Otherwise, you may die of a broken heart.

Set your mind on a goal, take care of today, keep your faith strong, and you will realize your dream.

CHAPTER 3

THE CYCLE OF NEEDS

SECURE IN OUR HOMES

> Each day of human life contains joy and anger,
> pain and pleasure,
> darkness and light, growth, and decay.
> Each moment is etched with nature's grand design.
> Do not try to oppose or deny the cosmic order of things.
> ~*The Art of Peace*~

MOST OF US WILL NEVER SEE A ROOM OF GOLD BARS, let alone luxuriate in the wealth. Many of us, at this moment, live in less-than-abundant circumstances. Many as dire as Admiral Stockdale's. How does one rise above the conflict and noise? How does one prevail despite the odds? Why do people strive to better themselves?

It is in our nature to provide shelter and food for our family, to bring them love and belonging. We show our love by giving gifts, by providing for our loved-one's needs. Self-fulfillment comes from sharing successes with others. It is also in our nature to wish for a better life and to want respect and recognition from other people. We strive to fill our lives with comfort and accomplishments, but self-enlightenment, according to Maslow's hierarchy of needs, is the point of ultimate human happiness.

Abraham Maslow was an American psychologist born early in the 20th century. He was interested in what motivated people, and how people fit into society while finding their personal happiness. He studied people he considered had far exceeded their calling on this earth: Quantum People. Mahatma Gandhi, Abraham Lincoln, Thomas Jefferson, Eleanor Roosevelt, and other leaders who held characteristics he admired and who he felt had attained self-actualization. Maslow developed his Hierarchy of Needs theory by studying how people achieved success in their lives. He believed there was no set rule for reaching self-actualization; for everyone this is different. It could be painting a picture, composing a song, or running a mega corporation.

Philosophers have written on the topic of self-realization for centuries. Is this state reserved for philosophers only, for people who live a noncomplicated life without strife or envy? If optimism and setting an end date is not the answer, what is?

Maslow's theory states our basic needs are physical, safety, belonging and love, self-esteem, and self-actualization. He arranged these in a pyramid because he believed basic needs must be in place before the next set can be met. As an example, consider a family sitting at the table for an evening meal.

The needs met in this simple homey scenario are these:

Physical: Food, air, water, sleep. A starving artist must eat and sleep, otherwise, where is the art? Homeless people strive to meet this single need, devoting their entire day to finding the next meal, and the next place to sleep.

Safety: The goal of safety is freedom from fear (Burger, 2004). The family sitting at a meal feels secure and stable. The family structure gives them a sense of order in the world, and they bask in the protection of the group. People living in a war zone are not safe, whether in an actual war, bullies dropping their bully-bombs, or an abusive parent. When people are not secure, they become distrustful and vigilant of others and distracted from the next set.

Belonging and love: Friendship, family, and love.

The desire to belong; to have a stable relationship and a supportive family. This is perhaps as strong as wanting food and water. If you feed a baby but leave him in isolation without human love and contact, he will die from failure to thrive.

Older people also frequently die in this way after losing their friends and family. An older person who is alone senses people don't care because they are "old." If you relegate your elderly mother-in-law to the back room with little human contact, she will succumb to a broken heart.

> He will hunger for affectionate relations with people ...
> for a place in his group or family.
> *~Jerry Burger~*

Self-Esteem: Perceiving oneself as accomplished. Achieving admiration and respect among family and peers. Self-respect and accomplishment are core human values. Self-esteem ties into love and belonging, safety, and being well-fed. Satisfaction with oneself leads to the next step.

Self-Actualization: People strive to meet their potential. You know who you are, what your dreams are, what you "want to be when you grow up."

> A musician must make music
> a poet must write
> if he is to be ultimately at peace with himself.
> What a man can be, he must be.
> He must be true to his own nature.
>
> ~Jerry Burger~

Dinner is on the table, we have a secure home, our family loves us, and we are healthy and happy. The need for food, water, safety, love, family, respect, and productivity lie within each one of us. These basic human requirements are necessary for sound mental health and a productive life. What more could we hope for?

What drives some of us to climb tall mountains, while others, most of us, are relegated to the flatlands of the city? The highest height many of us climb each day is by elevator to the job.

If the sense of security in our homes was at the top of the pyramid, we would not have scientists, leaders, musicians, and the other people who give human existence its richness. If the hunters/gatherers were happy with their lot, they would not have looked for ways to improve their situation, and we would still be picking berries for food.

The drive for self-improvement is as strong as the physical requirement for nourishment. Rather than a hierarchy, Maslow might have done more justice by putting the needs as a cycle. Life is not static. Life has many highs and lows, and sometimes we have little control over what happens to us. We cannot control other people, and sometimes we cannot control ourselves.

What holds us back from living the optimal life, the life of our dreams? What drives some people to great heights of achievement, while the rest of us flit somewhere in the middle? We can become so broken down from the disappointment of not meeting our dreams that we miss opportunities available to us in the present! If you don't have the drive, if you don't do the action, with all the talent in the world, you will never be an artist.

Maslow believed a peak experience happens when a person transcends time and place without anxiety, and has a sense of unity with the Universe. "A momentary feeling of power and wonder" (Burger, 2002). Peak experiences feel like a visit to a "personally defined heaven." We see heaven in art and hear it in music. Beethoven wrote by the voice of God. Children with autism seem to have an uncanny connection between their artwork and the Universe.

There is also another type of peak experience - one more accurately described as a "personally defined hell." Admiral

Stockdale turned his situation into a defining moment. It is impossible to live fully and not encounter strife. At least once in this lifetime, ill will in the form of strife and travesty will knock on everyone's door. The defining moment is not the ill will, but how one recovers from the upset and carries on. When forged by the fire, one learns to appreciate the beauty; the finer things in life. And appreciation for beauty is on the path to enlightenment.

Hobson's Choice, the Stockdale Paradox, and the Cycle of Needs. We have basic human needs, but the choices of meeting them are usually more practical than optimal. We make the best of our day, deal with the reality, and wonder if we will ever realize our personal dreams.

Herein lies the difference between the Quantum People and the masses. Quantum People transcend life's realities and live to talk about their experiences. They do not lose sight of their goal, despite the setbacks.

Optimism must be realistic.
You will never become an elephant
if you were born a mouse,
no matter how hard you wish it.

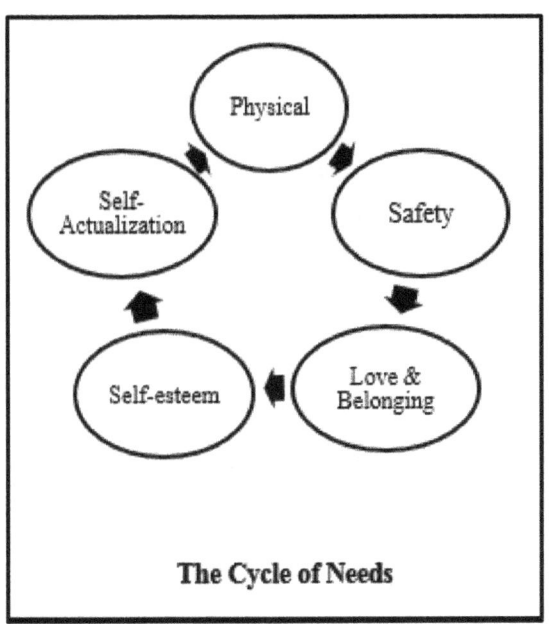

CHAPTER 4

POSITIVE SELF IMAGING

TAKING ACTION

Create each day anew
by clothing yourself with heaven and earth,
bathing yourself with wisdom and love,
and placing yourself in the heart of Mother Nature.

~The Art of Peace~

POSITIVE THINKING IS MORE THAN A THOUGHT PROCESS. Thinking and memories are complicated mechanisms. We store memories from the moment of birth, but we do not recall most of them. Even though infants and toddlers do not have a spoken language, these preverbal impressions shape perceptions that last a lifetime. Our adult actions and behaviors are directly related to our original, preverbal thoughts.

The problem is that many of our early perceptions are false. This is not saying memories are not real, but until about age five, children do not have the words to express what they are feeling. A mindset is developed from thoughts drilled into the subconscious mind. A child will take full responsibility for something she has no control over. Convinced she is responsible for the situation, any idea or possible alternative that challenges this belief is immediately dismissed.

If you want to change a part of your life, you must develop awareness of your perceptions. If you want to change your thoughts, change your viewpoint. As a child, you acted with a child's mind; as an adult, you must see your childhood from an adult's perspective.

At the click of a thought, you can go from anger to compassion, from hate to love - by changing your mindset. Stop for a moment. This won't be difficult. Your most angry thought is right beneath the surface, dwelling in your brain. Why are you so angry? Feel the anger. Not too much anger, though. If you are too angry you will see red and won't be receptive to the next point.

Now. Think positive thoughts about whatever you are mad about. Your anger is most likely toward another person, so look for something positive. Look at your anger from their point of view. Put yourself in their shoes.

You are not convincing yourself you are right and they are wrong, or heaven forbid, they could possibly be right, and you are wrong. Maybe you are both right and fully justified. Maybe this person annoys only you and doesn't share your anger. Whatever the case, consider the person as a person. Who are they? You don't have to analyze them, just find something positive you can understand.

Once you reach the point where you can see one inkling of good in this individual, stop and notice how you feel. Bask in the moment. What can it hurt? You aren't admitting to anything, just looking at the situation from a different point of view.

How do you feel now? Has the anger dissipated? This exercise should have taken the edge off your anger and created more pleasant thoughts. Do you notice a difference in the way your body felt? Less tense, lower blood pressure? Are you less angry? More compassionate?

We are bound in our justified anger and lose sight of the fact that there are always two sides to a story. We become angry for many different reasons, but behind that curtain of anger lurks the real answer: Exasperation, annoyance, irritability, indignation, rage, outrage, aggravation, resentment. When slighted and misunderstood, we show one of these faces of anger.

It is natural to want approval from our mothers, not a flaw in our personality. It is natural to want love and appreciation from those around us. When our basic needs aren't met, we become angry. We are so angry we don't even know why.

Here are descriptors of anger: "makes my blood boil;" "gets my back up;" "makes me see red;" "rattles my cage."

Anger does all this, and much more. Anger puts the body in a state of constant stress. Once anger grabs hold, the mind hangs on as if life depended on it. When we are angry, we ruminate and perseverate, as if riding on a merry-go-round. The residue of our anger never leaves us. Thoughts plague us day and night and make our lives miserable.

Happy is the opposite of mad. It goes to reason the angriest people are looking the hardest for happiness. And the harder they look, the unhappier they are.

The Quantum People agree; your thoughts lead your life. Have angry thoughts, you lead an angry life.

A newborn baby is in the most natural human condition. A baby is receptive to everything. This new world is so fascinating! Curiosity abounds. An infant, in his complete and total innocence, is at the ultimate peak of self-fulfillment.

The baby is not sweet and innocent for long. A stressed-out mom, arguing parents, and mean siblings eventually cause the baby's natural state of self-actualization to break down.

First, the child loses his self-esteem. "Bad boy!" Why is he bad? Doubts begin to erode his confidence and he second-guesses his natural tendencies because he is "bad." Once a child begins to doubt and mistrust himself, he doubts and mistrusts those he loves the most. After all, they are the ones telling him he is bad.

Doubt and mistrust threaten his sense of safety, the love relationship he has with his caregivers, and his communication with his basic self. Having lost touch with the pure infant who first appeared in this world, he tries to rebuild his self-esteem. When he becomes a man, he is scarred and bruised from the long journey of growing.

Positive thoughts, compassion, and understanding bring us back to our natural state. This is where the road forks for those who live the Quantum existence and those who do not. Quantum People have a connection to the universe, whereas the rest of us have blocked those channels with our negative, angry thoughts.

One cannot think straight when angry. How can you connect with the Universe in this state? Impossible! But positive imaging is more than simply right thinking. If you dream of being fit and trim, but are out of shape and sit on the couch all day, you will never be fit and trim.

He helps those who help themselves.

He who helps himself is the only one who can get off the couch to accomplish his goal of being fit and trim. Eating chips, drinking soda, and having zero activity is not the path to a healthy body. To become healthy, one must apply work to muscles and brain, and eat nutritious foods. This analogy points out the key for success:

THOUGHT + DISCIPLINE = ACTION

You must have the discipline to do the action if you are going to realize your goal. Thoughts will never get you off the couch.

Attaining self-esteem is easier when broken down into steps. Meeting goals is difficult without a stepwise plan. Good intentions, visualizing, and positive thoughts will only get you to your goal if you know where you are headed.

Gaining self-esteem, losing weight, becoming less depressed - it is wrong to assume you naturally know how to do these things. You are not a failure if you cannot make your dreams happen. You are not a failure, and you do not naturally know how to accomplish your goals.

Without a process or a formula to help reach your goals, you will encounter false starts and stops, never getting the project off the ground.

We meet goals by taking small steps.

See the end before you start, visualize where you will end up before you arrive: This is where dreaming, imagination, and positive imaging come into play. We would still be pushing rocks if our forefathers had not used their imagination and discovered the wheel.

THE SECRET TO SUCCESS

Thought + Discipline = Action

Positive Imaging + Action Steps = Reaching Your Goal

HOW TO DEVELOP A POSITIVE SELF-IMAGE

1. **When you have critical thoughts about yourself, stop and find something positive.** Like the anger exercise of finding compassion for someone else, give yourself the same consideration.

2. Begin your day alone. Wake when the house is still sleeping. Soon you will look forward to being up twenty minutes earlier than everyone else just to enjoy the quiet. Find a routine of meditation and gentle exercise to start the day off right. Connecting with the real you each day is necessary to boost self-esteem.

3. **Stop seeing yourself as a prisoner.** Examine your thoughts and your situation to find out why you think this way. Most people are trapped in this life in some form or another. Why are you trapped?

4. **Think of other people instead of yourself.** Show concern for others, learn to listen with patience. Connect with the speaker, not just hear the words.

5. **Show empathy and compassion** and people will shine the same back to you tenfold.

6. **Learn to live with yourself.** Enjoy you as your own best companion. You do spend all of your time together! May as well be pleasant and loving.

7. **Know yourself and what makes you happy.** Take time to learn who you really are. What are your core values? What are the beliefs that define you as a person?

8. **Practice gratitude daily.**

CHAPTER 5

THE TALKING STICK

LISTENING WITH EMPATHY

You would think such tall trees would require very deep roots. Actually, redwoods have a very shallow root system, designed to capture all the surface moisture possible. These roots spread out in all directions, and as a result, all the roots of all the trees in a redwood grove are intertwined. They are locked together so that when the wind blows or a storm strikes, all the trees support and maintain one another. That is why you almost never see a redwood tree standing alone. They need one another to survive.

~Norman Vincent Peale~

IT IS A SAD FACT. After millions of acres of forests have been destroyed, scientists discovered trees communicate both above and below ground. Colonies of fungi carry messages through the soil between the trees. Above ground, trees put out chemicals to warn the others when attacked by insects and disease. The scientists also found the oldest trees in the middle of the forest are the motherlode, and are the heart of the sustainability of the entire communication network.

Communication. Even plants communicate. Animals communicate. Not in words, of course, but however they do it, they seem to have no trouble in getting the word out.

Words. Plants and animals do not use words but they communicate. How did early humans express their needs before they discovered they could talk to one another? Communication is more than words. Turn off the sound of the TV and watch the actors. Have you ever been to an opera where the singers speak a foreign language? Even without understanding the words, with the richness of the music and the acting, the story unfolds. Words comprise very little of the communication process.

Consider your nervous system the same as a tree. To illustrate the pathway of our nerves, consider how the branches and roots spread out in all directions - green neurons sprouting new growth. When you prune a plant and cut off its new growth, the branches reroute themselves and continue to grow. When a brain is injured, new neurons grow next to the injury in much the same way, rerouting the impulses to another part of the brain to do the same task.

Like trees communicating with other trees through their branches, neural networks in the human body play a major role in empathy. Mirror neurons reflect feelings. Chemicals warn us of love or danger. A listener who is warm and affectionate reflects those emotions back to the speaker. A release of dopamine enhances pleasant sensations when engaged in a lively conversation (Ivey, Ivey & Zalaquett, 2014). Emotions are a combination of chemicals and neuronal networks.

Words are a small part of the communication process, and yet we use them so unjustly. Our emotional state is unconsciously expressed in our reactions; thoughts are reflected in our body gestures and facial expressions (Ivey, Ivey & Zalaquett, 2014). For instance, someone expressing fear drops their eyes downward, looks away, and talks quietly. This behavior is universal. Fear reads the same across any culture. A smile is a smile. A laugh - unmistakable in any language.

The basic emotions that guide us are *sad, mad, glad, scared, surprise, disgust,* and *contempt*. Not surprisingly, these emotions come from an inbred need for self-protection. Disgust is a protective factor telling us to not eat rotten or poisonous food. We are disgusted at the smell of excrement because odors warn us away from danger. We become sad when we lose our protection and belonging. Sadness is expressed with feelings of abandonment, rejection, anger, and depression. Emotions also have a positive side. Surprise can be a startle response to danger, but it can also be pleasant. We are shocked! Yet we can be pleasantly surprised.

There are also social emotions: *guilt, shame, pride,* and *embarrassment* (Ivey, Ivey & Zalaquett, 2014). Our basic emotions are formed at a deep personal level; social emotions are reflected in our interactions with others. Embarrassment and shame involve people, we feel pride in our accomplishments when we receive accolades from those who respect us. We feel guilty when we treat someone wrong.

THE NONVERBAL LANGUAGE OF EMOTIONS
(Ivey, Ivey & Zalaquett, 2014)

SAD	The mouth curves down, upper eyelids droop. Slumped body, drooping shoulders. Soft and slow vocal tone. Hunched with crossed arms.
MAD	Upright body, frowning, loud or forced tone of voice. Tense mouth and jaws, tight lips. Clenched fists. Hands on hips. Rapid foot tapping. The "Anger Grin." Might move aggressively toward you.
GLAD	Smiling, relaxed, open body posture. Direct eye contact. Leans forward, uses open gestures with the palms up.
SCARED	Tension and increased breathing. Averted eye. Furrowed or raised eyebrows. Bites lips, crosses arms, fidgets with fingers. Stammers or clears throat. The "Fear Grin."
DISGUST	Wrinkled nose, pursed upper lip as though smelling a stench.
CONTEMPT	An attitude of disdain and disrespect. A raised chin appears to look down on others. One corner of the lip is raised in a sneer.
SURPRISE	Eyes wide open, raised eyebrows, a crinkly forehead. Expression lasts only a few seconds. Tries to cover up the surprise.

Many early, native cultures used the Talking Stick in celebrations and council meetings. When the tribes gathered and had treaties and other serious conversations, the only person allowed to speak was the one who held the Talking Stick.

Once the speaker was finished, the Talking Stick was passed onto the next person who wanted to speak. In this way, the "ball" of the conversation was handed off from one person to the next, and only one person could speak at a time.

The listeners respectfully listened because they knew when their turn came, they would receive the same courtesy. Listening without interrupting also gave people time to quietly deal with their emotions. Since they couldn't interrupt, they could sort out what they wanted to say beforehand.

The Native cultures used this method to solve conflict. Thus, the name "Peace Pipe."

Listening is an art. Attentive listening communicates understanding and empathy. Listening is a skill. One that can be honed and sharpened. "Listening to myself" is not listening to others. When your mind is working on what to say next, you cannot pay attention to what the speaker is saying.

Attending behavior is a listening skill. Consider a conversation that didn't go well. How did you respond? What was the other person saying on a nonverbal level? If a component of communication is missing, the conversation will not go as expected.

RULES FOR USING THE TALKING STICK

- ~ Use appropriate eye contact.
- ~ Speak calmly, use a pleasant tone of voice.
- ~ Stay on track with the conversation.
- ~ Listen for main ideas.
- ~ Be aware of body language.
- ~ Listen with empathy.
- ~ Recognize the power of emotions.
- ~ Understand facial expressions.
- ~ Find positives and strengths in the conversation.
- ~ Listen with intention.
- ~ Pay attention to your responses.
- ~ Ask open questions.
- ~ Reflect feelings with more than words.
- ~ Let the speaker finish speaking.
- ~ Do not interrupt.
- ~ Think before you speak.

If emotions rule us, then why do we intellectualize the spoken word? When a person is upset, their emotions show in tone of voice, eye contact, verbal tracking, and body language. What is your first clue that someone is happy or sad? By their words, or their facial expressions?

Micro-expressions are emotions that quickly flit across the face, and then form into the social-face. Facial expressions tell the first thought that crosses a person's mind. Within seconds we sense whether we can trust someone or not. We unconsciously read their micro-expressions and body language. Friendly body language ensures trust. When two people trust each other, they face one another squarely and lean into the conversation. Pleasant facial expressions and appropriate hand gestures are signs of trust. When you distrust someone, you pull back, look down, and fidget with your hands.

Listening with empathy means finding positive attributes and strengths of the conversation. A respectful listener will keep the topic on the right path by asking questions and reflecting feelings.

How do you draw someone out and start them talking? The kind of questions you ask can either start or stop a conversation. Conversation stoppers are cold, closed questions using words like *"do, is, are"* requiring yes, no, and one-word answers. *"Do* you like me?" No. *"Is* the sun bright?" Yes. *"Are* you male or female?" If you want someone to start talking, ask them open questions. Questions that require a response instead of a grunt.

"Why, what, how, could?"

Another way of letting the speaker know he is heard is through reflection of feelings (Ivey, Ivey & Zalaquett, 2014). This can be expressed by confirming "I know how you feel," nodding the head, or repeating back to them in your words (paraphrasing).

One must be careful. Timing is important. A misspoken word can change a mood in a flash. A child takes your intent wrong, and he cries. Reflect to the waitress she looks great today, and she will give you great service.

Communication. It can sink ships and win wars. Words are powerful, yes, but even more powerful are the actions and emotions behind them.

THE FOUR COMPONENTS OF ATTENDING BEHAVIOR

1. Appropriate eye contact. The eyes are the gateway to the soul, so watch the speaker's eyes. Much can be learned by watching the eyes. However, different cultures regard eye contact in different ways, and this is where understanding comes into play.

2. Pleasant and smooth voice quality. A dog knows if he is in trouble by the sound of his master's voice. It is the tone of voice that sends the dog running, not the words. Communicate with a warm voice, and show interest and respect. The best way to win an argument is to agree in a respectful, strong voice. Agreeing with someone usually puts them off their guard and changes the direction of the conversation.

3. **Stay on the subject.** Verbal tracking means staying on task with the subject. How annoying to speak and have the listener interject a thought that has nothing to do with the topic at hand. Staying on the topic tells the speaker you are willing and happy to hear what they have to say. When someone is heard and appreciated, they are more likely to negotiate.

4. **Use comfortable body language.** Listening comes from the heart. An empathetic listener hears with the entire body. Instead of "thinking" with the brain, "feel" from the heart.

CHAPTER 6

YUIMARU - RECIPROCITY

HELP THY NEIGHBOR

The Art of Peace is medicine for a sick world.
There is evil and disorder in the world because people have
forgotten that all things emanate from one source.
Return to that source and leave behind
all self-centered thoughts, petty desires, and anger.
Those who are possessed by nothing possess everything.

~The Art of Peace~

HAVE YOU EVER BEEN SO UPSET your mind is churning, but when you open your eyes and look around, nothing has changed? Your environment, the people, everything is still normal, everywhere but in your head. A perfect storm.

Thoughts racing, your mental world is in chaos, but outside your skin - "normal." People cannot read your thoughts, they do not share your anxiety. When you are locked in this perfect storm, you are alone.

When a photographer reframes a picture, he zooms the lens in or out, or slightly changes the angle of the shot. Reframing thoughts work the same way. You can focus on a problem and look at the minute details, or step back and look at the big picture.

Each view lends a different perspective on the problem, and by combining it all together, a solution appears.

During the perfect storm we see only one point of view, and our mind tries to solve a puzzle without all the pieces. The thoughts of "don't-care, desperation, and despair" set in. It is moments like these when we touch our soul, when we are closest to who we are. Dark times test our mettle, our strength, our worth. People who live through this darkness proudly declare, "I've learned something about myself. I am closer to the person I want to be."

Why must we encounter travesty and drama before we can appreciate the finer parts of life? Art, music, love; beauty balances and manages the bad with the good, but we often miss appreciating these things until they are taken away.

Giving thanks will lighten a rotten mood. What are you grateful for? The beauty in your life! The people you love, the sun, the sky, your pet. Gratitude releases calming, pleasurable feelings that help clear the brain and relax the body. Once calm, it is possible to take a step back and look at the situation from another point of view.

The brain and body are happy to comply with anything you tell it. Whenever a negative thought creeps into your day, reframe the thought with gratitude and appreciate the beauty surrounding you.

This next exercise may be easier for some than others. Ponder horrible thoughts. Tell yourself how useless you are, how nobody loves you, life is horrible. How do you feel? Horrible? Worthless? Unloved? Relish the feeling.

Now think gratitude. Find five things you are grateful for; love, beauty, accomplishments. How do you feel? Loved? Accomplished? Isn't it remarkable how the mind can react so strongly to a thought? Recall this mindset often.

Eustress is good stress. "Eu" as in euphoria, eustress is pleasant stress on the body, like running a challenging race. The body is under stress, but the endorphins are pumping, and the high is close to euphoria.

Distress is the bad stress. Dis - lack of good; a malfunction. Disease - lack of ease. Distress - malfunctioning stress. Mishandling distress evolves into full-blown stress. And no high to go with it. Just a heaviness, the exact opposite of how you want to feel.

People must enjoy worrying! Stressing about something we cannot change or resolve occupies most of our waking hours. We refuse to sleep and choose to worry instead!

Quantum People accept the good with the bad. Even scarred and worn down, they radiate an aura of command, kindness, and confidence, forged through their tribulation. They show resilience; they put their past behind them, let go of the pain and suffering, and turn their experience into a life-defining moment.

People living a quantum life do not spend time ruminating over what happened in the past. Like the monk, they set down their worries and stop carrying them.

THE TALE OF THE TWO MONKS AND THE BEAUTIFUL WOMAN

Two monks were traveling in the rain, the mud sloshing under their feet.

As they passed a river crossing, they saw a beautiful woman, finely dressed, unable to cross because of the mud.

Without a word, the older monk simply picked up the woman and carried her to the other side.

The younger monk, seemingly agitated for the rest of their journey, could not contain himself once they reached their destination.

He exploded at the other monk!

"How could you, a monk, even consider holding a woman in your arms, much less a young and beautiful one. It is dangerous!"

"I put her down at the roadside," said the older monk. "Are you still carrying her?"

~The Book of Five Rings~

Resilience is the ability to bounce back, to recover quickly from a difficult situation. The number of protective factors that are present, or lacking, in one's life often indicate how a person rebounds from difficulty. Protective factors promote healthy growth. A strong sense of safety and belonging encourages positive thoughts and social connections. Risk factors, on the other hand, are those circumstances in life that compromise healthy development.

PROTECTIVE VERSUS RISK FACTORS	
PROTECTIVE FACTORS	**RISK FACTORS**
A positive temperament Intelligence Parental support and monitoring Decent schools Strong community networks Positive relationships with competent people A positive environment	A negative attitude Disabilities Academic failure Family conflict Poverty Lack of social networks Lack of emotional control Peer rejection A difficult environment
Risk factors can be overcome. If a child is living in poverty, a positive temperament and parental support will help weaken the confines of a difficult environment.	

Some of the oldest living people in the world, the Okinawans, set an excellent example of resilience. Okinawa is the main island of the Ryukyu Islands, a chain of many islands south of Japan. Ancient travelers called these tiny islands "the land of Shangri-La," and the Okinawans claimed their home as a peaceful paradise; *horai-jima,* "the land of immortals," a Shangri-La.

The Okinawans are living proof: How we live our lives affects our longevity; what we eat, how we act, and believe. While Western medicine is disease-focused, Eastern medicine uses herbs and spirituality for prevention of disease. The Okinawans combine the two; preventive medicine from Oriental thought, western medicine to cure diseases - but the rates of heart disease, stroke and cancers are virtually nonexistent in centenarians in Okinawa, and they rarely utilize western medicine. Interestingly, the younger Okinawan population with Western habits have an increase in these "Western diseases."

The Okinawan lifestyle promotes wellness. Their secrets for longevity include taking personal responsibility for their health, and having a strong social network where they gain strength from others. Living a balanced lifestyle is nature's way, and the Okinawans do this by nurturing their qi, or life force. Evolutionary biology says humans can live 120 years. The Okinawans prove this is possible. An elder in Okinawa does not live their final years in a nursing home sick and debilitated. They are healthy and vibrant, and surrounded by family and friends.

Aging in Okinawa is held in high esteem. If you touch an older Okinawan you share in their good fortune, health, and long life. The elders are revered. Their birthdays are celebrated throughout the village with parades and healing rituals. Women are recognized for their spiritual bonds between modern society and the past, and an older woman's clarity of wisdom is highly regarded and respected.

The strength of the Okinawan people lies in their treatment of others. They call this *yuimaru* - reciprocity. "Help they neighbor." The Okinawans have an extraordinary faith in mankind, and hold the opinion that people are inherently good. An individual is personally responsible for correct action, but if someone is failing, others are obligated to help.

Yuimaru, or reciprocity, is common among people worldwide. A fond memory of my childhood was when a member of my farming community died at harvest time. The farmers stopped their own harvest and spent a weekend bringing in the man's crops, the women laid out the food, and the children had a wonderful time playing together.

These types of social connections extend lives and protect us from illness. Positive social connections foster positive emotions. People with positive emotions and a sunny outlook have fewer illnesses and more friends.

The Okinawan recipe for longevity and resilience is simple. Nutritious diet, daily exercise, low stress, and integration of eastern and western medicine. Their diet is low-calorie, plant based, with unrefined complex carbohydrates. The easy lifestyle and happy outlook reduces stress; exercise and meditation play critical roles in their lives (Willcox, Willcox, Suzuki, 2001).

Unlike their American counterparts who may grudgingly trudge their way to the gym, if at all, the Okinawans make exercise, such as gardening and walking, a part of their daily routine. Okinawa is home to one of the most famous martial arts in the world, Karate. Tai Chi is also a common practice among Eastern civilizations. The martial arts are more than an exercise in self-defense, they help us connect to nature, to our spiritual self. By daily cultivating this healing energy, the Okinawans are also cultivating a longer life. Strong social connections, regular mindful exercise, a simple but nutritious diet, and a positive mental outlook. Despite their setbacks; wars, invasions, captivity, and oppression by the Japanese, the Okinawans remain hardy and irrepressible, and enjoy the benefits of a healthy mind and body.

Reciprocity is a universal truth. "Do unto others as you would have them do unto you." No matter what language, no matter the culture or religion, treating people respectfully is a philosophy that extends across the world.

In today's world, with the wars and riots, and disrespect for our earth and one another, people must practice reciprocity more than ever.

Herein lies the answer to peace. Treating one another with the respect and dignity that is our birthright.

Reciprocity, empathy, compassion. These three words are the same. You cannot return a favor or mirror an emotion unless you are empathetic to the other person's situation. Empathy breeds compassion. Once you empathize and understand, you can act in another person's best interests - with compassion.

Acceptance and compassion are not the same thing. You can understand someone's behavior without accepting it, but you can only change a person's mind by appealing to their deepest values. A person's behavior tells their story of hidden hurts and unrecognized worth. Remember this when dealing with an angry or abusive person - the times we must practice compassion.

We must also show compassion to ourselves. Self-compassion means to find sympathy for your hidden hurts, bringing them in the open and recognizing them. We quickly brush over this step because hidden hurts are painful. Locked away in their tight little containers, it is easier to tamp down the glimmer of pain and stuff it away then to look at the reason for the hurt and acknowledge it. It is difficult to show compassion to others when you have little for yourself!

Compassion for self makes us healthy and productive. Confidence activates a love for humanity which in turn allows you to love better and create value for the people you love.

Self-compassion makes a person feel valuable. You become stronger and less vulnerable to the negativity, and realize it is not necessary to have your opinion validated by others. It is easier to connect mentally and emotionally with other people when your mind is not riddled with doubts and fears. You recognize and accept what you cannot or do not want to change in yourself, and open the door to change the things necessary to walk on the path of self-actualization.

Self-compassion is powerful. Once clear on personal values, we can act in the best interests of other people. Power comes from focusing on the behaviors you want, both in yourself and others. Focusing on positive behaviors brings out the good; negative focus makes the situation worse.

If you want to be loveable, but harbor anger and resentment, then reframe your thoughts with compassion.

CHAPTER 7

A MAN OF PEACE

WHAT IS ZEN?

> Zen is to make you wonder, and to answer that wondering with the deepest expression of your own nature.
> ~Myomoto Musashi~

IN TODAY'S WORLD with the hustle and bustle, fast cars, speedy communication, and media overload, how can a person find the time, energy, or mindset to meditate?

Meditation brings us close to nature, but our lives today are not centered with nature. No wonder so many people in our fast-paced society give up on the idea. Meditating works best in a quiet space, free from interruption, and for many people this is difficult to find. When you do make the time and space, you feel better for it, but this is not an easy practice to stick with.

Meditation simply is. When in a meditative state, a person becomes closest to who they are. The pathways of energy open and you become one with the Universe. We are the Universe.

> The Buddha said, "Look within, thou art the Buddha."
> Jesus said, "The Kingdom of Heaven is within you."
> ~Myomoto Musashi~

Another universal truth. Our greatest power lies within.

How do you tap into this great power? Amid our busy, stressful lives, we realize we should sit and smell the roses each day and take time for ourselves, but this hard to do. It takes time and discipline to focus the mind and achieve a calming meditative state.

For meditation to effectively fit into your busy life, it must be quick and something you can do anywhere. The difference between mindfulness and meditation is this: During mindfulness, by paying attention to the details, you consciously notice what is happening within and outside of the body by focusing on the present. Mindfulness reminds you to be consciously aware. Meditation, on the other hand, works on the unconscious level by priming energy and restoring the body - without conscious thought.

Meditation is the direct path to finding what lies within us. Whether it be Buddha or the Kingdom of Heaven, or both, meditation (and prayer) are the mediums to reaching both heaven and within.

It takes practice. Bodhidharma, the Buddhist monk who taught the Chinese the first martial arts, meditated in front of a cave wall for nine years. The original Buddha, Prince Siddhartha, sat in contemplation for years before he discovered the Great Truths. This was the beginning of Zen, a life filled with meditation and rightful living.

The main philosophy of Zen centers on abandoning the ego, which simply means to replace thoughts of righteousness and pride with humility and grace. The previous chapters in the book suggest ways to do this. Compassion, reciprocity, listening with your heart. Ego does not play a role in peaceful negotiations nor peaceful living.

> Abandoning the ego is the secret of right living.
> In life, as in the practice of the martial arts,
> it is important to strengthen the will
> and develop strength and skill.
> But the main thing is to strengthen the spirit
> and find freedom
>
> ~Taisen Deshimaru~

There are two types of meditation: Active and passive. Active meditation is what you do in your everyday life, which we will discuss further into the chapter. Zazen is passive, or sitting, meditation; by sitting quietly, you can clear your mind of thoughts and just be. Zazen is the path to Zen, to enlightenment.

Sitting zazen was also the way of the mighty samurai, the *Bushi*, the elite class of warriors of feudal Japan.

Japan was a powerful country between 1500 and 1600 A.D. During this time Japan made its conquest of surrounding lands; Korea, China, India, and the Spanish Philippines. In 1600 A.D., the Tokugawa clan became the rulers, and for the next 300 years Japan was completely isolated from other countries. Until the Tokugawa era, the practice of Zen was reserved for the upper class, the Buddhist monks, and the samurai warriors.

Over the years, different Shoguns massaged the ideas of Zen until it became a people's meditation. The Tokugawa period was a time of peace and prosperity for the Japanese, and Zen flourished among the people.

The disciplined samurai was a core element of the Japanese culture. A warrior must learn to control his reactions in the most stressful situations known to man. When faced with death, one must keep a cool head. Without morals and values, a warrior is a stone-cold killer. The Japanese, as brutal as they were in their wars, realized their samurai had to have exemplary character.

Training for a samurai was long and arduous. Young boys learned to meditate for many hours at a time. For discipline, the teacher used a *kyosaku*, a bamboo stick frayed on one end. An errant or inattentive student would be whacked with the *kyosaku* to bring him back to reality - or in this case - Zen. This practice brought enlightenment and developed strong qi.

> Your master is teaching you exactly the right way
> to cut your mind free
> and find the truth you are seeking.
> ~*Taisen Deshimaru*~

Cut your mind free and abandon the ego.

Japan's most famous samurai never fought in a war, but won his fame by sparring with other wandering samurai. Myomoto Musashi was born in 1584, near the end of the reign of the Japanese warlords. Born into the warrior society, the *Bushi,* Musashi was raised with the rigid discipline of the samurai. Feudal Japan was undergoing massive social changes. They had conquered the surrounding lands, and except for the insurgents in Okinawa, the wars were over. The samurai became jobless. Comfortable with living at the top of the class, with the dispersing of the Japanese army, the displaced soldiers were reduced to wandering the countryside looking for employment.

Theses rogue warriors, or *Ronins,* kept their skills sharp by challenging one another to duels. Musashi was a *Ronin.* The wars were over, so at age 13 he took his skills on the road. For the next 17 years Musashi fought over sixty battles and won them all! He used whatever he had at hand; long sword, short sword, knife, boat oar, tree limb; whatever was handy at the time.

When he turned 30, he realized swordsmanship was more than just a fighting skill. Musashi put down his sword and began to study Zen in earnest. He sculpted wood and metal, and painted the open spaces of nature in a style called Sumi-e. He held the conviction he could do anything and he did not have to be taught how to do it, because he believed his knowledge arose from within. He called this Heiho.

The essence of Heiho is to build an indomitable spirit and iron will,
to believe you cannot fail in anything.
The true path of Heiho applies to any time and situation.

~Myomoto Musashi~

In 1643, when Myomoto Musashi turned 60, he wrote *The Book of Five Rings*. Originally written as a letter to his student, Musashi's book outlined his thoughts on the way to enlightenment. In this five-chapter book; Earth, Water, Fire, Air, and Emptiness; Musashi reveals what he learned during his lifetime regarding swordsmanship and a strategy of life. He felt life should be practiced with the precision of a swordsman. To Musashi, the secret to success was strict discipline of thought and action. This knowledge of rightness does not come from an outside ethereal source, but from an internal limitless source - within you.

Musashi believed any obstacle can be overcome with proper behavior, living, and strategy. His belief and his words carry over 400 years, with the legacy of his ideas ringing true even today. In many business schools and war colleges across the globe, Musashi's *Book of Five Rings* is required reading.

Living in the past or the future causes anxiety, worry, fear, guilt, regret, and anxious anticipation. "Stopping mind" is when we become caught in our thoughts and the mind stops to question, decide, or judge what to do. When this happens, we lose track of what is going on around us.

When first beginning meditation practice, the mind wants to stop at every thought. Have you ever taken a shower, stepped out, dried off, and realized you did not remember the showering experience? Did you find you were busy planning your day, ruminating over a fight with your wife, wondering how you will manage your defiant child?

This, and more, can easily pass through our minds in the time it takes to shower. Our mind stops at our thoughts, and we do not enjoy the water. Universal energy, or qi, is much the same as the water.

Continually flowing, qi doesn't stop when we stop paying attention. We stop our minds and miss the flow, just like we miss our shower.

Zen is not complicated. It is what we do every day. Breathing, eating, sleeping. Doing what comes naturally.

How do you practice Zen in our fast-paced, hyperactive world? Who has the time to sit for forty minutes a day to cultivate a clear mind?

Practice is the key. Through practice, the brain, body, and mind learn to respond more quickly, until the response becomes truly a response, and not a conscious thought. With practice, entering Zen becomes a habit, and a way of life. If you practice a behavior until it is forgotten to the subconscious, when the time comes to use the technique, you do not have to think about it.

A beginning musician practices the scales over and over to develop familiarity with the piano so the fingers will strike the right keys. Over time, the songs grow harder and the rehearsals more intense. After years of perfect practice, the act of playing the piano sounds natural and not practiced. The people listening are unaware of the long hours of preparation it took to sound effortless.

This is Zen.

Zen is not a mystical, heebie-jeebie, unobtainable exercise for the privileged. Zen is in everything we do.

> When you sit, just sit. When you eat, eat.
> Approach the situation for what it is and nothing more.
> Whether you like it or not is irrelevant.
>
> ~*The Book of Five Rings*~

The object of meditation is not to have a mind completely empty of thought - impossible for most of us. The object is to listen to your breathing and have relaxing, calming thoughts, instead of the every-day worries and confusion. The deeper into meditation, the easier it is to recall this relaxed state at will. With practice, when you are in the middle of a stressful time, when the body is hot-wired for the stress reaction, you can be calm.

Rearrange your schedule so you have thirty minutes, alone and uninterrupted. To do this, you can leave for work earlier and stop along the way; stop on your way home to unwind from the day; or rise sooner than the rest of the house. Take time to relax for a few minutes without being bound by the clock.

When you first start to meditate, acknowledge your monkey mind, and allow your thoughts to stop wherever they choose. After a few minutes of this mind-stopping activity, give your mind a rest. Stop thinking. Tell yourself no more ruminating or worrying for the next ten minutes. As time goes on, it will be easier to calm your mind on command.

At first, a timer is helpful. Use a timer you can set and forget, not a clock you have to check. Eliminate as many distractions as you can.

Meditation is not meant to be difficult, the pomp and circumstance surrounding it are rituals to make it seem more meaningful. You can burn candles and build shrines, or you can sit in your car with a cup of coffee. It is up to you.

As you practice, make the sessions longer. Do this calming exercise whenever you have the chance. You will resurrect a state of relaxation simply by breathing deeply.

Congratulations, you are on the road to abundance.

> From one thing, learn ten-thousand things.
> ~Myomoto Musashi~

WHAT IS ZEN?

- ~ An approach to life.
- ~ A way of life.
- ~ A philosophy of iron will and spirit.
- ~ Not a religion.
- ~ A set of values and beliefs.
- ~ Responsibility for self.
- ~ Self-reliance and profound honesty.
- ~ A strong work ethic.
   "No work, no food."
- ~ A practical discipline.
- ~ Strengthens the power to cope.
- ~ Enhances compassion for self and others.
- ~ Helps realize your potential.
- ~ Reduces the ego.

HOW TO MEDITATE

"Visualize the Breath"

It is important to breathe properly when meditating. Whether sitting Zazen or practicing active meditation, concentrating on breathing enhances the flow of qi. Counting keeps your mind from wandering, and also helps with relaxation.

1. Clear your mind and take a deep belly breath. Calm your thoughts. Next, put your left hand over your lower abdomen and cover it with the right hand. You are covering the core of your being. The dan tien, the area three to four inches below the naval, is where our vital energy is stored.

2. Breathe in through the nose for a count of four, visualizing the breath going to your hands, stop your breath for four counts. Imagine a fire building in your belly. Feel the warmth.

3. Release the breath through your open mouth for a count of four, imagine the negative thoughts and toxic energy leaving your body as you push out your air. Hold for a count of four.

4. As you inhale, stoke the fire; see the flames blaze. When you exhale, see the smoke follow the path of qi throughout your body. Visualize the energy flowing in a great circle, up from the dan tien to your head, and back around again. Concentrate on your breathing and your visualization.

Moon Over Still Water"

Sitting Zazan and in a quiet meditative state, imagine a full moon shining on a mountain lake. Feel the breeze, hear the sounds, become the moon, the lake. Feel the awesome quiet. The lake represents your mind. Calm and still. The moon is your life, shining brightly. Feel the sensations and relax.

"Follow the Qi"

An active meditation that involves both mind and body.

1. Do this meditation outside in a quiet place, if you can. Clear your mind. Take a breath. Calm the thoughts. Next, stand up tall, and place your hands over your lower belly and begin meditating.

2. Keeping your hands clasped in front of you, breathe in and feel the world around you. Hear the sounds, connect with nature. Become one with the world. Let the wind blow through your body as if you were a void. Let the wind take your troubles away, dispersing them in the air. Imagine you are not "human," simply another being on this earth.

3. Raise your hands to the sky, arch your back, feel the power of the earth, become a conduit between heaven and earth.

4. Place your hands near your shoulders, and as you bend down, push your hands down along your chest, abdomen and legs, visualizing pushing those dark, toxic thoughts away from you into the ground.

5. Reach for fresh earth, feeling the healing power and renewed energy as you run your hands up the backs of your legs, your back, over your head, and into the air, feeling energized and refreshed.

6. Repeat this, reaching to the heavens, pushing the dark thoughts out of your body into the ground, bringing in golden energy from the earth, up your body and into the heavens. All the while, concentrate on your breathing, feel the flow of qi coursing through your body. You will know it when you feel it. A tingling, exhilarating, goose-bump kind of feeling.

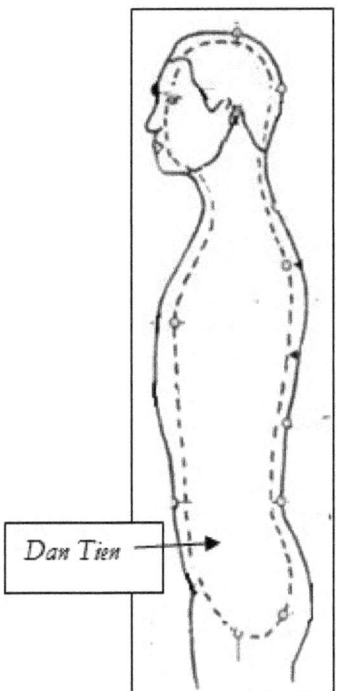

Follow the qi from the dan tien, up the spine, around the brain, down the face and chest, and back to the beginning.

Learning to direct one's qi is necessary for self-healing. After becoming proficient at visualizing the flow of qi through the body, the next step is focusing qi to heal pain. Imagine the flow going to the hottest point of the pain and gently massage that area with your mind. An internal (psychic) massage, so to speak.

This technique is also useful for ridding the mind of toxic thoughts. Visualize the qi circling around in your brain picking up all your troubling thoughts, and when you exhale, see them disperse into thin air.

If you are satisfied with yourself

you are humble and peaceful

CHAPTER 8

FAITH AND FORGIVENESS

RELEASE THE GRUDGE

Whoever says to this mountain, "Be removed, and be cast into the sea;" and does not doubt in his heart, but believes that will be done; he will have whatever he says.

Whatever things you ask when you pray, believe that you receive them, and you will have them.

When you stand praying, if you have anything against anyone, forgive them, so that your Father who is in heaven may also forgive you.

If you do not forgive, neither will you be forgiven.

~Mark 11: 23-26~

THIS PASSAGE SHOWS A VITAL CORRELATION between forgiveness and faith. To move your mountain, you must have faith. To have complete faith, you must first forgive. Is this to say we must forgive the people who placed this huge obstacle in our life? How do you forgive someone who purposely sets out to destroy you?

Faith is a universal truth; a belief in something unseen and unknown, greater than ourselves, "a complete trust or confidence in something or someone." Admiral Stockdale had complete faith he would overcome his hardship and prevail in the end. He had faith, but he also had the discipline to take care of his daily tasks. *Do not confuse faith that you will succeed with the discipline to face your most brutal reality.* Just as thinking will not get you off the couch, faith alone will not get you to your goal. You must also use discipline to take the action necessary to get there.

Faith extends far beyond a place of worship; it is something people draw on many times a day.

THE FAITH FORMULA
DESIRE + BELIEF + EXPECTANCY = FAITH

Desire - you must want the goal with all your heart.
Belief - you must believe you deserve what you want.
Expectancy - without a doubt, you expect to achieve your goal.

If your faith is not strong, you are lacking in either your desire, belief, or expectancy. You may have doubts about the outcome, or your desire is weak. Using the Faith Formula, you can find the weakness in your faith, and build it stronger.

Strong faith is only half the battle, forgiveness is the other half. Isn't the purpose of forgiveness to let someone off the hook, let bygones be bygones, and bury the hatchet? All's well that ends well, so to speak. No. Forgiveness is none of these.

The point of forgiving someone is to free your soul so you can get on with your life. Forgiveness means to stop being angry or resentful towards someone for an offense or mistake; no longer angry or wishing to punish an offense.

To be forgiving is to show mercy, compassion, caring, patience, tolerance, and understanding. You do not absolve someone for what they did to you, and forgiving is not saying you are happy with them. When you forgive, you are willing to look at what happened from another point of view, accept the wrongs against you, put them behind you, and get on with your life.

Once you forgive the person who wronged you, the pain dims in importance. Forgiveness goes much deeper than taking a mental health vacation. The Universe does not work in a negative state, and harboring ill feelings toward someone is a negative state.

If you want your bully to go away, silently forgive him. Remember the exercise earlier in this book when you found understanding though compassion? When the Universe hears your compassion, opportunity will come into your life.

Holding grudges blocks opportunity. Your mind cannot see goodness because you are stuck in the black hole of hatred.

Forgive and let the Universe do the work. Honestly release the grudge, and see the conflict resolve on its own. It takes a leap of faith to forgive and let go, but if you want your turmoil to resolve, this is what you must do.

Faith, forgiveness, and spirituality are linked together. Faith is believing, forgiveness is letting go, and spirituality gives us strength.

Spirituality and religion are not the same, but they are the same. Even though one must be spiritual to have religion, spirituality extends beyond the capacity of religion. Religion is when a group of people believe in a common Supreme Being and come together to worship in collective harmony. This also gives them the opportunity to socialize and establish networks, and fulfills the need for interaction with others that is a necessary part of human existence.

While early humans were inventing the wheel and mapping the stars, they also believed in a Being greater than themselves. Early cultures relied on many gods until the Hebrews spread the word of the existence of only one God. Half of the world's religions today (Judaism, Christianity, and Islam) are based on this ancient teaching. The other half of the religions have their beginning with the Hindis in India, which then spread into Asia, and developed into religions such as Taoism, Shintoism, Confucianism, Buddhism.

These are the values of all the religions of the world:
~ Reciprocity.
~ Gratitude.
~ Compassion.
~ Faith.
~ Prayer or meditation.

> ...there are many differences in how people around the world conduct their religious rituals, but philosophically and spiritually, Christianity and Islam closely resemble Hinduism, Taoism, Buddhism, and Confucianism.
>
> Cultural and language differences give the Supreme Being different names such as God, Allah, Brahman, Primordial Lord, or Buddha who is held in esteem as our Provider and Savior, and will reward us with a place in Heaven.
>
> ~*Master Wong Kiew Kit*~

To resolve conflict, it is necessary to find a common ground, a place where all parties can agree. From the moment of agreement, people are surprised to discover they share ideas. Once the opposing sides realize they have more in common than differences, the conflict turns into friendship. Herein lies the answer to peace. What would be left to argue if nations agreed to disagree on the name of their God?

Religions offer the comfort of communal worship and solidarity in believing in the same way as others. Spirituality is believing in what you cannot see and understanding you are driven by something stronger than your conscious mind.

Quantum People understand they are ruled by something higher, something greater than themselves, and communicate with this higher power through prayer and meditation.

"Spirit" is the name we give to the harmony of body and soul - our psyche, the inner self. It is a state of mind, an attitude of morality and ethics, beliefs, and principles. Strength of character. Courage. Spirituality is believing in what you cannot see. What is within you.

Faith is for moving mountains. Forgiveness is for moving forward. Spirituality is the momentum that guides us. Three more gifts to carry on your journey to abundance. Faith, a light and grateful heart, and a guiding light to show the way.

AFTERTHOUGHTS

DO WHAT YOU LOVE

> Contemplate the workings of the world,
> listen to the words of the wise,
> and take all that is good as your own.
> With this as your base, open your own door to truth.
> Do not overlook the truth that is right before you.
> Study how water flows in a valley stream,
> smoothly and freely between the rocks.
> Also, learn from holy books and wise people.
> Everything - even mountains, rivers, plants, and trees -
> should be your teacher.
>
> ~*The Art of Peace*~

WE EQUATE ABUNDANCE AS LIVING WITH RICHES. Although we can find abundance wherever we are, we presume abundance and wealth go hand in hand. In our minds, to have wealth is to have abundance. It takes strength of character to live in utter poverty and believe you have all the abundance in the world. Money is necessary to meet the cycle of needs. Physical needs require money, as does safety. Love is giving, and the more you give, the more you show your love. We cannot help it, our self-esteem is based on the finer things in life; the better our living quarters, the better our mental outlook.

Obtaining wealth has the same mindset as any other success. You must desire, believe, and expect it before you receive it. You must act in a certain way. Most importantly, you must cancel the idea that the love of money is the root of evil.

Money is money, a means to an end. Money is not evil, just the people who spend it in evil ways. Banish the thought that having riches is wrong. When in tune with the Universe, you express the desires of the Universe. When the Universe is in control, abundance will freely flow.

If a room full of gold bars is your goal, then this is your Supreme Power beaconing you. Follow your heart. You will be amazed.

Taking the Quantum Leap is not jumping into another physical realm, a different reality. Rather you are leaping into another consciousness; another plane of existence.

Quantum People live a fulfilling life, but they are not in another physical realm, obviously. The ones who shine the strongest in our memory have strong moral character and cause great things to happen. They are the ones who set humanity on edge. True, some nasty characters spring up throughout history, but who are the heroes? Who are the ones revered the most? The longest remembered? Who gives the world the greatest legacies? The Quantum People! Those who transcended so-called human limitations and followed their heart.

True abundance comes from doing what you love. Surround yourself with beauty, with people who love you, follow your heart, and do what makes you happy.

With the body, mind, and soul in a row - when these three are aligned, then life is in perfect harmony. Success follows harmony.

Success comes from knowing what you want and having a blueprint as a guide to meet your desire.

Following your heart means following the voice in your head - the one telling you to go forth and multiply. Ideas. Opportunities. Multiply your ideas by believing with absolute faith you will accomplish your goals.

The thought is formed when you see it in your mind's eye. Apply action and the goal will become real.

Seeing and believing do more than help realize your goals, they also keep you in touch with the Ruler of the Universe. Uncanny events happen once you are connected. Have a worry, let it go, and the answer will appear. This is not nonsense. This is what happens when you take the leap into your true existence.

What you search for is right here, inside of you. You know what you want, your desires and dreams. These are not fantasies found in story books, but the Universe coming through, expressing your worth to the world.

If you follow those urgings instead of directing them, you will become spontaneous in your living and therefore more open to opportunities. Your inner voice is telling you to do this thing for a chance at an opportunity. "Try this idea, see how it works," the voice says. How many times a day do you argue with that voice; reason it out, tamp it down, tell it to go away, the thing cannot be done. Squashing ideas and opportunities for abundance.

One word of caution: Be careful what you wish for.

Be careful that when you throw out the old, you do not throw out your treasured blanket. Not everything in your life must go, does it? Keep the possessions and people who enhance your life. As you view your life in gratitude, you will find parts you do not want to change. Loved ones, possessions, even habits, and that is okay.

You may bring about drastic changes in your life; find another job; get married; get divorced; move half way around the world. Or there may be no visible change to your physical existence. The change, whatever your outer world, will come from within.

One day you will notice life is running smoother, amazing things happen without explanation; you are happier. This is when you will know you have taken the great leap into your quantum life, and have found abundance.

SKILLS FOR LIVING

- ~ Love one another.
- ~ Listen with your heart.
- ~ Understand certain choices are not really choices.
- ~ Treat others the way you want to be treated.
- ~ Everyone has the right to speak.
- ~ Thought + Discipline x Gratitude = Action.
- ~ Desire + Belief + Expectancy = Faith.
- ~ Meet your needs.
- ~ If you can imagine it, you can achieve it.
- ~ Unrelenting faith and forgiveness.
- ~ Meditate to keep the channels of the universe open.
- ~ Take care of today, no matter the difficulties.
- ~ Stay focused on your goal.

Abundance is everywhere.
Opportunity is limitless.
Neither have boundaries.
It depends on your point of view.
Peace, dear Readers.
May you take the Quantum Leap
into the life of your dreams.
Look inside, and you will find.

BIBLIOGRAPHY

Burger, J. (2004). *Personality*. 6th Ed. USA. Wadsworth.

Collins, J. (2001). *Good to great. Why some companies make the leap and others don't.* New York. HarperCollins.

Deshimaru, T. (1982). *The Zen way to the martial arts. A Japanese master reveals the secrets of the Samurai.* (Amphoux, N. Translation). USA. Penguin Books.

DeWall, C. N. (2013). *Scientific secrets for self-control.* USA. The Teaching Company.

Ivey, A.E., Ivey, M.B., Zalaquett, C.P. (2010). *Intentional interviewing and counselling, Facilitating client development in a multicultural society.* (8th Ed). Belmont, CA. Brooks/Co.

Lao Tzu. (1961). *Tao teh ching.* (John C.H. Wu, Translation). Boston, MA., Shimbala Publications.

Musashi, M. (1988). *The book of five rings.* (Nihon Services, Translation and Commentary). USA. Bantam Books. (Original work written 1645).

Peale, N.V. (1996*). Positive imaging: The powerful way to change your life.* USA. Ballantine Books.

Wattles, W. (2009) The science of getting rich. (original work 1910). USA. Penguin Books

Willcox, B.J., M.D.; Willcox, D.C. Ph.D.; Suzuki, M., M.D. (2001). *The Okinawan program: Learn the secrets to longevity.* USA. Random House.

Wong Kiew Kit. (2002). *The complete book of Shaolin.* Reprint 2012. Malaysia. Cosmos Internet Sdn. Bhd.

ACKNOWLEDGEMENTS

To Catherine, Florence, and Gwendolyn, my beta readers. Your input is most appreciated. A thank you to the men and women before me, authors all, who passed on their knowledge and legacy into the pages of this book. To my family, for their great patience and understanding. And to the greatest power, to whom I am deeply grateful for the expression of words that made this book possible.

ABOUT THE AUTHOR

The challenge of writing a how-to book such as this one is living the advice. Words flow easily onto paper, but how easy is it to live it?

Pickett's seal, "Chaos," reflects this book perfectly. "Out of chaos, a star is born." If life was ever in chaos, it is now. Out of that chaos, this book was born.

Pickett has degrees in healthcare, social science, and the martial arts. She lives in Wyoming and is raising her granddaughter.

Also by C.W. Pickett

*Walking Between
The Raindrops*

A Treatise on Trauma

~I was the prey,
I couldn't stay away~

C.W. Pickett

Mushin Press

WE LIVE IN A VIOLENT WORLD.

School shootings, mass murders, terrorism, child abuse.

Our early perceptions influence our choices as adults. Personal growth is limited by beliefs formed in childhood.

What compels us to do the things we do?
Is it possible to heal from trauma?
Can we break this hold violence has on our lives?
Can the demons of our past be put to rest?

Within these pages, you will find insightful answers to questions like these - and more.

READ THIS BOOK TO FIND WHY:

The past must be processed, not forgotten.
Abuse knows no boundaries.
Women stay with their abusers.

If you are living in trauma, this book is for you!

Together we can make a difference! Let's make our world a safer place.

7
Seven Summers of Stalking

**A WHITE PAPER ON
THE #1 CRIME AGAINST WOMEN**

C.W. PICKETT

Mu Shin Press

ARE YOU A VICTIM OF A STALKER?

Does someone repeatedly do any of the following to you?
- ✓ Follows or spies on you
- ✓ Sends you unwanted letters
- ✓ Makes unwanted phone calls
- ✓ Stands outside your home or workplace
- ✓ Vandalizes your property
- ✓ Threatens to kill your pet

This is the definition of stalking by the Department of Justice. If you can answer yes to two or more of these and say they happen on a repeated and regular basis by a person that is causing you a great deal of fear or annoyance, you are being stalked.

You are most definitely not alone! 7.5 million Americans, most of them women, claim to be stalked every year. Stalking causes lost work, estrangement, financial loss, and mental distress. Most stalkers never pay for their crimes.

Find inside:

"If you are being stalked…" checklist.

A section on cyberstalking.

READ NOW! THE MOST COMPREHENSIVE, UP-TO-DATE REPORT ON STALKING, THE CRIME THAT GOES UNNOTICED BY POLICE AND JUDGES. THE #1 CRIME THAT CAUSES GREAT FEAR AND HARM TO MILLIONS OF AMERICANS EVERY YEAR.

www.ingramcontent.com/pod-product-compliance
Lightning Source LLC
LaVergne TN
LVHW041631070426
835507LV00008B/565